THE QUICK AND DIRTY

GUIDE TO LEARNING LANGUAGES FAST

MYKEL HAWKE

Racehorse Publishing books may be purchased in bulk at special discounts for sales promotion, corporate gifts, fund-raising, or educational purposes. Special editions can also be created to specifications. For details, contact the Special Sales Department, Skyhorse Publishing, 307 West 36th Street, 11th Floor, New York, NY 10018 or info@skyhorsepublishing.com.

Racehorse Publishing™ is a pending trademark of Skyhorse Publishing, Inc.®, a Delaware corporation.
Visit our website at www.skyhorsepublishing.com.

10 9 8 7 6 5 4 3 2

Library of Congress Cataloging-in-Publication Data is available on file.

Cover design by Michael Short

Print ISBN: 978-1-63158-301-8
Ebook ISBN: 978-1-63158-302-5

Printed in the United States of America

CONTENTS

THE
PRELIMINARIES

AUTHOR'S PREFACE

Most species communicate, but only humans have developed their communication skills to the degree that they can differentiate complexities with intricate detail. People can then convey these communications in print, audio, video, electronic, or other forms. Likewise, as is our primary concern in this book, people can communicate these thoughts in other languages to serve them as they travel the world or interact in their own world with others who speak different languages.

Regardless of why and how languages developed and differentiated, they did so. We now have a world with a few very common languages and a vast multitude of less disseminated tongues that are, no doubt, just as important to those remote people as English is to the business world.

Whether a person travels for business, resources, knowledge, or just for pleasure, he must accept that his travels will require him to interact with other humans and that this interaction will require a common language to communicate. Therefore, before embarking on any foreign travel, any wise person would do well to learn enough of the language spoken in the area to be visited to enhance his experience.

I wish you all the best in your travels or studies, whichever the case may be. I only know that you can never go wrong using your time to study, particularly languages because they offer you the greatest opportunity to reach out and touch someone. But languages also provide you with an opportunity to be touched. This is life.

I hope you find this book to be as useful for you and your loved ones as I have found it to be for me and my "Brethren." Enough talking—I leave you with this thought, or something sufficiently similar, that I heard somewhere during my travels: "He who learns another language earns another soul."

—Mykel Hawke

FOREWORD

By Mykel Hawke

When I first wrote my book, *The Quick & Dirty Guide to Learning Languages Fast*, almost twenty years ago (printed in 1999) with Paladin Press, I really didn't have any expectations that it would get published. While I had hoped it would get picked up by a publisher, this was not the main reason I wrote it. I wrote it on a promise to myself on a day when I was almost killed five times!

I'll return to that story shortly. . . .

Now, almost two decades later, the book has remained in print, as it was a popular book within its genre and a bestseller for over a decade while it was with Paladin. Paladin was a small niche publisher specializing in military and mercenary type publications, since their owner was Special Forces Colonel Robert K. Brown. Brown was also the owner of *Soldier of Fortune* magazine, a very respectable alternative news source during the dirty little wars of the Cold War era.

Ironically, my language book was sold under their espionage category, which was always a source of humor to me, but it made sense. If you want to do that sort of thing, language was an important skill. As times have changed greatly in twenty years, Paladin closed its doors and permitted me to find a new home for the book.

That's where this updated version comes in. I am very grateful to Skyhorse Publishing for picking up the book. I am also grateful to my Special Forces brothers who helped me find Skyhorse—James Morgan Ayres, a published author and friend, whom I met through Jim Morris, another Special Forces Officer, author, and TV personality. I always like to give credit where due and looking back in hindsight, it's interesting to see how everything works out.

I'm writing this now, in my now-established traditional style of writing as I speak, and in hopes that Skyhorse will include this with the updated chapter as part of the backstory behind the book. I consider it a bonus anecdote for those who purchase this newer version.

Back in the nineties, I was a Senior Special Forces man, serving as a Medic, Commo, Intel and Ops, Sergeant First Class with JumpMaster and Advanced Non-Commissioned Officer school, and I received ratings in seven languages.

During that time, I had been sent to the very prestigious Defense Language Institute (DLI) to learn Russian, given that Russia was the enemy of that era. I graduated early with honors, achieving a "3/3/2+" rating, nearly as high as a nonnative could get. Ironically, the wall came down around the time I graduated and our unit shifted its focus to Latin America. With most folks in our unit only speaking Eastern European languages, that presented a problem and a challenge.

So, I realized I wanted to work there, but needed to learn Spanish quickly to do so. I had just spent a year in DLI and there was no way they would send me back for another long term at a school. During my time, I analyzed the English words I used and needed daily. Then, I made some charts and lists, and started to learn the Spanish words I needed, concentrating less on grammar, rules, conjugations of verbs, and tenses.

Grammatical foundations are good for taking a long time and building a strong base, but I needed function and fast. We had a deployment opportunity for a Spanish speaker to go to Honduras for three months to work as a doctor, dentist, and veterinarian, but we had to have at least a 1/1 level on the language assessment test to get selected. So, I created a system, used it to learn, took the language assessment test and scored 1+/1+, and then got selected to deploy.

I was then able to put my skills to the test by living, working, and treating locals in remote villages. During this time, I was only able to speak in their native language. I did this every day for three solid months. That proved to me that the system I had developed worked—and worked well.

Then there was an international incident where a US Navy ship fired a missile that struck a Turkish ship and killed five Turkish sailors in October of 1992. Consequently, our unit was tasked with training some Turkish Special Forces in the states and then accompany them on a mission in Turkey.

Needless to say, no one in our unit spoke Turkish, so I began studying. After thirty days, I was able to function as a very rudimentary interpreter for the duration of the mission. Later, I was teaching the method to one of the 18Bs (the Weapons Sergeants on the team) how to learn another language with the format. Another teammate, who was a university professor of language, asked if he could use my technique and told me I should publish it. But I didn't care about that then. I just wanted to learn, teach, serve, and complete missions.

After Desert Storm, I felt that war just wasn't enough for me, so I got out of the Army and began contracting, long before 9/11, and before everyone knew what that was. Back then, it was a very small community, coveting work in real war zones, and the competition was fierce. You would only be hired by word of mouth and reputation. Remember, the internet as we now know it was in its infancy then. There were no "job boards" online; this was all old-school, back-of-the-bar recruitment like the old black-and-white war spy films!

I started in the Azerbaijan gold wars for a year, speaking Russian, on a CIA contract. Next, I went to Colombia for a year in the drug wars, speaking Spanish, followed by Haiti for eighteen months as part of the transition of the US Military from Operation Uphold Democracy over to the civilians of the UN. While there, I worked with Russian helicopters and crews to communicate clearly to the world that the US Military had turned over power. During this time, we established a group called Argentine Quick Reaction Forces and, of course, the Haitians and UN folks spoke French. With my security men being former elite American military, I ran the operation speaking Russian, Spanish, French, and English fluently every day. I was promoted to country manager and under my leadership, we received the State Department's Small Contractor of the Year award in 1998.

After that, we were needed to help with the coup that occurred in Sierra Leone, West Africa. I was sent to be the country manager and run the aviation support of the war effort, in part because I had just proven myself as a leader and manager in Haiti, but also in large part because I could be counted on to be honest and never accept any blood diamonds. I later realized that, in part, is what kept me alive—I was known to be honest and could not be bribed by either side. They put a million-dollar price tag on our helicopters; I only had a ten-thousand-dollar price on my head.

They spoke English, so language is not part of this story; the near-death incident is. Remember when I first opened this chapter, I mentioned that I was almost killed five times in one day, and that day is what lead to this book. . . .

The war in Sierra Leone was quite frankly the most brutal and horrific of any of the conflicts I have ever seen. The rebels were known for their extremely violent and inhumane torture, mutilation, raping, burning and killing of men, women, and even children.

Like Colombia, the conflict was intense. In Colombia, we averaged being shot at three times a week, but it was always while we were in the air, eradicating drug crops and drug labs, and it was always clear who the bad guys and good guys were. But in Sierra Leone, those lines were heavily blurred, as most of the West African Forces wore a mix of uniforms, and the bad guys often dressed like civilians or in a mixture of uniforms. So, there were times, on the ground, when it was difficult to discern one from the other.

As a result of the confusion that prevailed on the battlefield, I was nearly killed three times in one day. That is another story for another book, but that was my record until the fall of Freetown, when the rebels took the capitol and utter chaos, death, and destruction ensued. We did our best to rescue civilians and citizens, but the rebels were running amok and were dressed like the people they were killing. On that day, I was nearly killed five times and broke my personal record.

However, it was the last event of the day that lead to this book, where I found myself surrounded by a group of rebels who wanted to make me into Swiss cheese with their AK-47s.

At that glorious moment, the fifth time of the day facing death, I thought for sure, *Myke, this is it—the day and the way you die.* In that split second, like a classic movie scene, I literally saw my life flash before my eyes and thought to myself: *What do you wish you could have done before you died?* Like a bad cliché, the answer that came back was, *Publish a book!*

So, there I was, facing forty rebels with AKs ready to shoot me and I smiled to myself. I think that smile is what made them hesitate. So, I saw a chance and pulled a bluff! I told them if they shot me, the chopper behind me would blow up and kill all of them! It wasn't true, but they didn't know that! They bought my story and in that moment, I pointed to the hangars and told them that the field a click over had hot food and cold drinks, and that they could all get cleaned up and rest. They were filthy. They bought it and started walking. I jumped on the bird and as we flew out I called the troops at the airport and let them know. They mopped the rebels up. Done.

So, from that moment, I decided I'd write a book when I got back stateside. My first six months back from Sierra Leone were rough. Dealing with some PTSD, I decided to live in the desert with my white wolf, Lukos, my jeep, my rifle, and just shoot, drive, and write. I wrote three books—a kid's book, a novel, and the language book. I sent each of them to three publishers of those kinds of books. Paladin picked up my language book and that was that. Mission accomplished; I forgot about it.

At that point in time, I was still contracting. Prior to Sierra Leone, while on a scout in Colombia, we had a bad aviation day and had three faulty aircraft in one day. The last one was a twin-engine plane whose engines both failed while over the mountains. I was with Special Forces General Harley Davis, and some other amazing Special Forces Leaders. I started cracking jokes, as I knew we were going to crash. We survived it and Harley had asked me to consider coming back to the Army and share my knowledge with the troops. I admired him and I decided to return to the Army, but this time, as an officer. Due to these factors, the language book was published under my pen name, A. G. Hawke.

Then 9/11 happened. I went to all the Special Forces Officer schools and into combat. When I returned, the media had a great interest in the Special Forces. Since I was working as a producer for ABC at the time of the attacks and I was running an adventure tourism and survival school, the media found me and that lead to me doing eight series, a film, and over fifty TV shows. Now that I am retired as of 2011, this book is now published under my publicly known name, Mykel Hawke.

I share all this now, because I can, having started as an unknown person back in 1999 and then having been blessed to gain some notoriety from media. So, for those folks who may find it of interest, since many people see me on a TV show or see one of my books, but don't fully realize how much real-world service as a soldier and experience as a contractor went into making those shows and books.

So, nearly getting killed five times in one day in Africa is what created this book almost twenty years ago. And since so much has changed, this section will be dedicated to sharing a lot of the new technologies and resources available to help you learn a foreign language.

It may be tempting to rely solely on the tech gadgets due to their prevalence, ease-of-use, and accuracy, but remember the stories I just shared. Only real knowledge in an emergency will save you when it matters most. So, use the tech, but do not let your life depend on tech alone. Learn the basic skills and no one can ever take that from you or deny you that skill.

The secret to learning a foreign language quickly is . . . use!

How does one *use* what they don't know? Learn it, but not the conventional way; learn it the *guerilla way*—that is, just the stuff that matters most, first.

If you were to analyze your own vocabulary in the course of a normal day with family, friends, and co-workers, you'd find you only use about two hundred words or so. So, why not focus on those so you can speak in another tongue?

I won't get too deeply into what nouns, verbs, adjectives, and adverbs are, or into a lot of grammar; those things are mostly for the other books. I cover the basics of the language to learn languages, as I like to jokingly say. But the bottom line is that what you need are:

- A handful of nouns—like the words for "people," "places," or "things"
- Then you need to learn a handful of verbs such as, "to need," "to go," and "to do"

- Then a handful of adjectives such as, "good," "bad," "big," "little," in opposites
- Then a few adverbs such as, "well," "poorly," "quickly," and "slowly"
- Then a few prepositions such as, "in," "out," "above," "below," etc.

Then you need to start with only two conjugations: "I want" and "you want," for example. How we say a verb so that it reflects the tense, person, number, etc. is called conjugating. Many languages have a root verb that changes according to who says it.

Our language does this a little bit—"I want" versus "she wants" is an example.

We're almost done! Next, you need a few key words that convey the sense of time. Words like "now," "later," "today," "tomorrow," "yesterday," "before," and "after" are great for most things.

Interrogatives are important. The questions "who, what, when, where, why, how, how much?"—coupled with a few pointing fingers and a map, pencil, and paper—can go a long way! After that, make a list of key nouns you'll need like "food," "water," "help," etc.

It never hurts—and always helps—to learn how to say "please" and "thank you." If you open every time with "please" and close with "thank you," no matter how badly you hack their language, they will know you are foreign and see you are trying and hear that you're polite and will help.

The last thing in the section, but the first thing you should do, is to learn the traditional greetings and phrases such as "hello," "goodbye," "my name is . . . ," "what's your name?" etc.

So, putting it all together, it may look something like this:

"Hello, My name is John/Jane. I need water. Where, please? Thanks."

Bam! Day one, you are speaking and communicating. Now, pick your language and let's look at some tools to help get you there. An hour a day is a good start.

There are many apps, CDs, DVDs, etc., which will teach you how to study and learn the language information you need, which I will discuss later in the book. However, there have been many advances in technology since this book was first published. I'll cover some of those advancements on the following pages.

If you have satellite radio or TV, try to find some content in the language you are trying to learn. Sirius XM Radio offers French and Spanish stations. Some satellite TV providers will let you subscribe to channels from other countries. These are great tools to help one learn a language.

I recommend watching some kids' shows in the target language. Buy some DVDs or a subscription to a streaming service such as Netflix or Hulu. Download shows to your phone or computer so you can watch while you are traveling or when you are not connected to the internet.

Of course, these days, one need only go to the internet and watch nearly any kind of show, or listen to any kind of music, in just about any language.

Even if what you hear sounds like machine gun rapid fire, the more you listen, the more your brain gets attuned and reprogrammed to pick it up. It's called "passive learning;" writing or speaking is "active learning."

There are also so many great applications for learning languages to download on your phone or computer. A lot will depend on whether you want a free one or to pay for one. Usually, the premium ones are free of advertisements and are well-made.

There are applications that can see languages with your device's camera, or hear folks speak into your phone, and translate it. These are *awesome*, but often very slow and flawed.

Another thing to consider is that if they are not connected to the internet, they oftentimes don't work.

When it comes to technology, Google Translate is one of the best. You can type in and translate over one hundred languages when you are connected to the internet and about half of those when you're not. It can translate more than thirty languages for practical uses, such as translating photos of signs, watching and converting live videos, or translating speech to language audio. It's simply amazing!

Microsoft is not quite able to stand up to Google overall; however, their real-time language translator is simply the best one out there right now.

SayHi is one of the better applications for speech-to-speech conversion and, in general, Speak & Translate and TripLingo are excellent tools on the market.

For Asian languages with their unique characters, there are some applications, such as Papago and Waygo, that specialize in these and are really good for native European language speakers.

Two products that are wicked cool are *wearable* translators, The ILI & The Pilot. The Pilot is of special interest because it's simply an ear bud that you wear almost unnoticeably, but it translates real time. They all have limitations, but they are way cheaper than hiring a personal human translator.

Finally, there are some photo-translating applications that allow you to take a photo of a sign or billboard, for example, and then translate it. These require internet connectivity, so they have some limitations for utility, but most signs will be in cities, or if not, you can type the letters in to your translator app when you're not connected and check your downloaded dictionary to figure it out.

Some of these photo applications are: Cam Translate, Quick Cam Translator, Photo Translator, and Word Cam, but the best of this genre is still squarely with Google and Microsoft.

While I do not work for any of these folks and do not want to favor any product more than another, there are a handful of sources I can say that I have used for years and as such, can speak to their efficacy from personal experience. It will be important to check yourself for technologies and products that are out there, as these will surely change frequently and will only get better and better as time goes on.

However, it is vital to understand that when I first started studying languages, there was no internet and a limited number of applications and programs for language learning. There were only books, teachers, and courses, and if you were lucky, they had tapes or records!

Please note that none of these applications should replace hard work and time spent to learn and understand a language. The worst-case scenario is that everything you own is lost; only the skills in your head will save your life. If you lean too heavily on the technology, you become dependent upon it and weaker at the skill. It's the same scenario as using a GPS and never using a map, or not memorizing key phone numbers and then losing your phone.

There is no replacement for real skill. Technology is a great tool, but you are your best resource.

As a survival guy, I recommend diversifying with technology and other language tools. It's particularly important to have applications that work offline. Additionally, always carry a tiny dictionary with adult words and a small phrasebook.

Often, a good person who sees that you need help can find the word in their language and then show it to you. This way, you can work it out together. However, this way should not be solely relied upon.

That being said, one of the very best ways for humans to learn a language is with a "Long-Haired Dictionary" and/or "Six Pack Dictionary," that is, another human being. One of the best ways to learn is with another person. Nothing motivates you better than to speaking to someone face-to-face.

Translators, financially or situationally permitting, are obviously one of the best resources. Whether you're using a translator for professional or personal reasons, it's important to *pay attention*. You want to learn from them while they speak, of course, but you also want to make sure that they understand you!

For example, if you offer a dollar to a beggar and you watch your "terp" or interpreter make mean gestures, and then see the potential recipient get angry or afraid, then you know something isn't right! It may be your terp is from a tribe that hates the other person and you just joined a war! Or it might be a simple misunderstanding and your terp asked for a dollar instead of offering one.

Which brings me to the importance of gestures. Some gestures can get your butt kicked, or get you in a fight and then land you in jail, where you may even be executed. A simple "okay" sign in America is calling someone an "asshole" in other countries. Do your homework.

Another thing that can actually get you killed is not studying the culture of the language you're using. For example, in some places, people get highly offended if you stop and ask a woman for directions. Be smart!

Coupling culture with gestures, learn the signs of other cultures if you plan to travel there. Not everyone uses US & EU style signage.

Also, some cultures yell as a way of communicating; don't take it personally and get offended. Please note, yelling doesn't make them understand you any better, so don't get frustrated and become the ugly American.

Learn and be patient, stay calm, expect mistakes, and have a good sense of humor. You'll get through it and may make some lifelong friends along the way, but for sure, with some language studies, your chances of survival will increase and you'll live to tell many funny tales!

While it's not 100 percent right for everyone, the Top Ten

list of important phrases and questions I've curated on the following page is a good starting point for anyone.

The first key to success in using this Top Ten is to choose the *easiest* one for you to learn and remember and then use the heck out of it!

These key phrases and questions were created to help you maximize use of the interrogatives, and to always use the polite words or phrases, such as "please" and "thank you," to cover any mistakes you make with general words associated with kindness. These are ways to ensure the maximum willingness and helpfulness from those you query.

The Top Ten Phrases to learn in any language are:

1) "Hello. My name is _____. What is your name?"
2) "I need help. Can you help me, please?"
3) "Can, would, or are you able to show me, please?"
4) "How do I get there or do that, please?"
5) "Where is that person/place/thing, please?"
6) "When is that or this, please?"
7) "What is that or what do I do, please?"
8) "Who can help or who is that, please?"
9) "How much" is best instead of "how long" or "how far" as you can always say "how much time," "how much distance," as well as the usual "how much cost?"
10) "Thank you" and "good bye," "until later," and "go in peace."

You don't need to ask for the time; you can look and see it. You don't need to ask about the weather; you can feel it. You don't need to ask complex questions because you won't understand their replies!

Seek simple ways to solve problems. Seek the simplest way to say it in English, then use the easiest way you can with their language in vocabulary that you know. Finally, seek simple answers so you can understand.

The key is to asking simple questions and getting simple answers is to stop trying to speak like you think in your native tongue. Take a moment and convert it to grade school vocabulary.

Listen actively and carefully, and then reply accordingly. Do not stop them or yourself. They may rattle off a lot of words; let them. By focusing on listening for the answer you seek, often, you can catch the key word you need. In doing so, you're letting your mind filter their response.

When you ride a bike, you don't think about it at all; you let your body just do what it does and it just knows. The same thing happens involuntarily with your mind. When I was taught Morse Code, we first learned the basics, but as the speed increased, our brains could no longer translate dots and dashes to letters. We had to stop thinking and let our minds just hear and translate, and suddenly, we were getting all of it, without thinking.

So, do the same with language: let them respond, focus on a few key answers you're anticipating, and allow the rest come together. You'll be surprised!

Then, there is the confirmation technique. You asked a question. They gave a reply. Now, repeat to them, slowly, and simply what you think they said. They'll correct you if you missed it or affirm that you got it right.

To summarize: if you use the rules I have provided for learning a few verbs, nouns, adverbs, adjectives, and a few other helper words like "now," "later," and "already," in conjunction with the Top Ten List of phrases and some modern translation apps, you can make significant progress in a short amount of time. After reading this book, if you spent one day writing down these words in your target language, listening online how to say them, writing down how they sound to your ears, and committing their sounds to memory, then you'll be able to speak the basics in a day!

So, learn a foreign language as a survival tool and do 'Merica proud!

Note: I was rated in seven languages by the Army and was paid for three, the maximum allowed at the time. I'd like to point out, I still brutalize Russian, Spanish, and French, especially with french people, and I happily admit I mainly speak English and Bad English. I studied many other languages in my three decades of serving and contracting.

INTRODUCTION

There are many reasons why you might need to learn a foreign language quickly, as well as many reasons why you might not have studied one before. None of this is really pertinent here, except to point out that there are many ways of learning another language, but very few seem to be truly fast and effective.

The reason I developed this quick and dirty method of learning a foreign language is that, as a Green Beret, I had to travel to many countries on short notice on vital missions with complex requirements that required me to work intimately with foreign officials in a professional capacity. Regardless of how hard I searched, I could never find one book or method that got me where I needed to go in the time I had to get there.

For my first foreign language, I was trained at the Defense Language Institute (DLI) in Monterey, California, where I learned the basics of study. The DLI teaches some very difficult languages, and quickly, to a lot of people, but it still operates on the premises that it takes 6 to 18 months to learn a language and you always begin at the beginning and proceed step-by-step through the course.

The real world, unfortunately, has some rather unreal demands and expectations, and Special Forces have to operate in the real world. But they don't call us "special" for nothing. We are just regular guys who rise to the occasion, adapt to the situation, and overcome the obstacles. Being quiet professionals, Green Berets don't quibble when given a mission. We just set about accomplishing it.

So I decided to tackle the problem of quickly becoming proficient—or at the very least adequate—in a language the Special Forces way. One of the first things you learn as a Green Beret is to stick to principles as much as possible. Techniques are variable, depending on the situation, but principles hold true through it all. So, when Uncle Sam came to me and told me to take this, go there, and do that, I stuck to the principles. I assessed the situation and decided that I couldn't learn the languages quickly enough with the instruction I had available. I needed to modify the program and adapt it to the specific needs of the mission. The adaptation came in the form of throwing everything out and starting over.

This technique violates the principles, you say? In fact, it doesn't. It sticks to the K.I.S.S. principle—keep it simple, stupid. You don't need to build a fortified defensive position when what is really needed is quick shelter from the storm! Or, in this case, if you don't need to practice law in the tongue you're trying to learn, you don't need to spend five years studying the ancient dialects to get ready to begin studying the language.

To develop my specialized method of instruction, I built backward, the way you're supposed to plan. First, I figured out what was needed and then how to get it as quickly and efficiently as possible. Using this method I have become officially rated in seven languages: Russian, Spanish, French, Italian, German, Serbo-Croatian, and Turkish. I used many of these languages within weeks of beginning to study them and served as the official interpreter on our missions. In addition, with a little research and effort, I was able to create summaries for the other members of my Special Forces team so that they too could function with a day of study.

From these summaries, I wrote this book so that you could learn a foolproof way of conquering a foreign language. It works for any language—from the more common Romance languages, such as French or Spanish, to the more exotic tongues, such as Arabic, Russian, or Japanese. For the less familiar languages, you will need to select and use a very good guide or dictionary in conjunction with this guide.

You know your mission, whether it's for travel, business, or just speaking with a friend. Your objective is to conduct your mission in the language required. Your goal is to obtain the instrumental tool needed, which is the language itself. Your parameters are to do all this in the time allocated. Reasonably, I suggest one week to one month.

Now that you have all this lead-in and everything has been spelled out clearly in military-style terminology, let's discuss a few details about my quick-and-dirty method of learning a language before we get operations under way. The basic premises taken for this book are as follows:

- You were not raised speaking more than one language.
- You have not had the opportunity, or perhaps the desire, to learn another language.
- You have either never had formal training, or you have found it inadequate for your needs.
- You need, for whatever reason, to learn a foreign language quickly.
- You need to be functional in the language, but perfection is *not* your immediate concern.

No amount of time and money could ever be set aside to train everyone in everything they might ever need. Yet, the very success of missions frequently comes down to the ability to communicate in a language different from our own. No books, no schools, no courses ever seemed fully up to the task . . . until now.

Do not kid yourself: you still acquire a language the good, old-fashioned way—you have to *learn* it. But here I have trimmed the fat for you and gotten down to brass tacks. No fluff, all action words, so you can get into the action yourself.

Now, let's do it!

OVERVIEW

This overview will help you use the methodology in this book most efficiently and effectively. The concept is quite simple: get rid of everything that is not absolutely necessary and then focus on the most useful tools to get the job done. That is what you will be doing shortly.

First, you will prepare yourself by getting your equipment ready. Second, you will organize yourself and the use of your time. Third, you will embark on your route according to the plan provided. Fourth, you will apply yourself regularly and test yourself daily to note deficiencies and determine your focus. Fifth, you will build on this foundation and implement your plan by using these "word" tools every way you can.

You should pay special attention to the "Learning Tips" scattered throughout the text for your convenience and listed at the back of the book. These are the quick secrets to learning a language quickly and effectively.

By the time you've followed these directions, completed the outline, filled in the blanks, used the words, and applied your imagination and creativity, you will be speaking the language you have chosen to learn. It will happen. Envision it. See yourself speaking it. Hear yourself speaking it. You are mere steps away.

Bon voyage!

BEFORE YOU BEGIN

Watch movies, read children's books, listen to music, and go to restaurants to get an insight into the culture and nuances of your target language.

To really learn a language fast, there are some techniques that I find more helpful and enjoyable than those used in old-fashioned—and harder—methods of study. I think you'll enjoy these accelerated methods as well. The key is to immerse yourself in the desired language as much as you can. To do that, it helps to get into the culture as well.

1. Think like the people who speak the language natively, act like them—it will help immensely.

2. Find music of that culture and in that language and listen to it as much as possible.

3. Watch movies in the language as well. Subtitles help a lot but are not critical. You are trying to get a feel for the language: how native speakers stress and where they stress, their intonation and annunciation of syllables, etc. Study their mannerisms and gestures. This is a tremendous—and pleasant—method of determining if their language is animated or subdued. These subtleties will clue you in as to how to interact more propitiously with the natives. This, in turn, will make them respond to you more favorably, thus encouraging you to continue your studies and encouraging them to assist you—which ultimately will serve to enhance your overall learning.

4. Eat in their restaurants. Try to order food in their language.

5. Look in your local papers and find their cultural events. Attend them and make some acquaintances who might be willing to help you with the language.

6. Of course, listen to the CDs or tapes you acquired as much as possible (e.g., in the car on the way to work or whenever you can fit it in). Bombard yourself with your new language. Tell yourself you love it, even when you're sick and tired of it. Smile, breathe, and keep listening.

7. Read kids' books, newspapers, and magazines in that language, and surf the 'Net. By the way, kids' books are wonderful tools for learning a language. Don't be embarrassed. Remember that you're on a mission—once you're rapping in the lingo, it doesn't matter how you got there. You will appreciate your skills, and others will also.

8. Find a friend (maybe a romantic one if you're single) who does not speak English very well, because if he or she does you will revert to the language that is easier for both of you. To begin your study, you'll need a few tools.

YOUR LANGUAGE TOOLBOX

1. Get a good writing pen and notebook that you can dedicate to this one language. (Because the forms at the back of the book are reproducible, you might want to use a three-ring notebook instead of a bound one. This way you can take the pages out whenever you like, organize them however you wish, and put them back. Plus, you won't have to carry the whole notebook if you don't want to, only the lessons you need for that day or specific situation.) You will carry the notebook for a while, use it a lot, and save it for a long time, so be sure to buy a high-quality one that will last through the abuse it's bound to receive.

2. Next, you will need at least two books for the language you want to study: a dictionary and a phrase book. If you are going to be traveling, the smaller these books are, the more likely you are to carry them, and if you carry them, the more likely you are to use them. If you're not traveling, buy the biggest, nicest dictionary you can afford because you will learn much more from a large dictionary than a smaller one.

The phrase book is a bit trickier to select because anyone can make and sell them—and they often do. You do not need a book that will teach you how to say, "I would like to go to the market and buy a nice, fresh, pink piece of pork," or "Can you fix my flat as it seems to have been damaged by a nail?" No doubt, there may be a time when you might need to say one of these phrases, and there is probably at least one person out of every million people who would express themselves in this way. However, what is more suited to your needs is to find a phrase book that gives you common expressions that serve a variety of purposes.

The concept behind acquiring tools is simple. Yes, you can buy a very expensive tool set with gadgets galore that were made specifically to fix other gadgets, and although they might be handy once in your life, they otherwise take up space and cost money. You need very few tools that will fix most anything. Then, if you decide you need more tools because you like "mechanicking" or you just have to keep working with tools, you can slowly acquire more as needed. The same applies to your language tool kit. Seek those words and phrases that will give you the biggest bang for the buck, the ones you can use the most.

Choose your phrase book based on this concept. Take a few moments and look through all those available to you. Shop at a few stores if you need to. Look for the basics, such as greetings and terms of politeness. Then look to see if everything is broken down into categories:

food, medical, directions, etc. The books should give you the words by themselves and then the phrase that you'll most likely use. The simpler the phrase the better because you can combine phrases or add and subtract words more easily without making grammatical errors that might make you quite incomprehensible. I have found Barron and Berlitz phrase books to be the best. Again, you are going to write down phrases you think will be useful in your own study book.

3. Another useful tool, but one that may not be so easy to find, is a set of flash cards or a grammar book. The flash cards are often available for Romance languages, but if you can't find them or don't want to buy them, make your own. You can learn more words faster and reinforce learning as you go. The commercial flash cards and phrase books are usually called the "fundamentals of Spanish," or whatever language they are about. Each foreign-language phrase book or dictionary usually has a grammar section in it, so you might not need to buy a separate one. Find one that breaks the language down to its simplest components.

A really neat trick for learning the grammar of another language is to do just like children do—get a kids' grammar book for that language. Grammar will tell you how to put the sentences together the way they do, as well as those little things you need to know for each group of words such as tenses, cases, and conjugation.

4. An optional tool that is quite helpful if you have absolutely no idea how the language sounds is a compact disk (CD) or tape. Again, use your best judgment based on the above-listed criteria for selecting these. The "rain in Spain falls mainly on the plain" is nice to know but doesn't mean much when you need help on the streets. (And you can make your own tapes or CDs as well. This is cheaper and

allows you to tailor them to your needs. Plus you can alter them to reflect your progress. When making the tapes, be sure to leave a pause after each word or phrase to give you time to pronounce it.)

Since most people learn better by visual means, books are more the focus of our orientation here. However, some folks find it easier to study with audio aids. If you do, apply the same techniques and schedule outlined here for books.

The principles are the same: find the tools and study. The techniques are up to you. You know yourself, so adapt those that work best for your personality.

Now let's learn a few key words. . . .

KEY WORDS FOR WORDS

I know, I know, you're dying here and saying, "I have to learn grammar terms! What the heck! Over?!" No worries, these terms are mostly for you to read once and basically forget. Most of them will be readily apparent to you or will refresh your memory from school.

The primary reason for this section is so we can have a mutually agreed upon foundation and point of reference. There are a few techniques that will require you to know some of the terms listed below so you can apply them to the way you construct a sentence or phrase. Likewise, if you find yourself studying another language or continuing your study of the same one later on, you'll find these very helpful.

So, let's look at a few key words for words!

Adjective—The description of the noun (e.g., smart, big, expensive).

Adverb—Describes the verb itself (e.g., slowly, quickly, over, under).

Learning adjectives and adverbs is greatly enhanced by learning them in opposite pairs (e.g., hot/cold, quickly/slowly).

Antonyms—Words that are opposites, such as *good* and *bad*, *hot* and *cold*. (Learn as many of these simple words as you can, and you will be able to put them with one verb and one noun and convey just about everything you could ever want or need. The trick is to always think about what you want to say, very quickly and then shorten it to its simplest construction. "The food is good / the food is bad" will serve you very well. You might not be able to tell that it is good because you love garlic or bad because you're a vegetarian, but the basic thought is conveyed.)

Articles—In the English language, *the, a,* or *an* tells us if something is specific or general. Note that many languages, such as Russian, do not have articles.

Case—The name for the general rule that causes declension is case. In English, if something is just there, doing nothing and nothing is being done to it, this is nominative case just because it's there. If something is being given to something or someone, this is accusative case because one is the direct recipient of action from the other. There are many names for cases. Each language will have its own cases and rules for them. The point here is that you should have an idea what these words like *case* mean, so you can read the rules yourself and know what is being talked about and not be lost in terminology.

Learn to use cognates to maximize your useable vocabulary.

Cognates—Cognates are words that are related by descent from the same ancestral language and usually are similar enough that you can recognize what they mean simply by looking at the root. For example, passion is *passion* in English and French; the English *to pass* is *passer* in French, close enough to know what it means by the way it looks and reads and often by the way it sounds once you've learned a few things about your desired language. Many Latin words have cognates. Even the most complex ancient languages or the simplest, rarest, or most remote languages also use them, especially with regard to modern words such as *computer* and *telephone*.

Conjugation—Learning conjugation is challenging because you must learn the rules for changing a verb to match the pronoun and the tense. For example, in English, we usually just say the verb or add the letter "s," such as *I give, he gives*. But many other languages have a separate ending for each pronoun group.

Conjunctions—Conjunctions are just what they say they are—words that join, such as *if, and, but, or*.

Declension—The inflection of nouns, adjectives, and pronouns; the change of the ending undergone by these sentence parts to express their different relations of gender, person, number, and case. This is when a root word must be changed by the rules to reflect a thought. For example, in Russian *dom* (pronounced dome) is *home*. To go home is *domoy*. Hence, in English we would use the word *to* to convey the thought; in Russian the word itself is changed based on the verb used with it and the rules of that verb. This concept is called *declension*.

Gender—Some languages confer a gender to each noun such as masculine, feminine, or neuter, and the articles or adjectives must reflect this (e.g., *el hombre*, not *la hombre*.)

Gerund—Verb forms that function as nouns. In English, gerunds end in "ing" (e.g., swimming, running).

Imperfective—A verb form or aspect expressing that the action is ongoing and therefore not perfectly and simply completed. For example, "I was reading the book while he was cleaning."

Interrogatives—Absolutely the most important words to learn initially, interrogatives are the questions: *who, what, when, where, why,* and *how.* In a foreign language they can say so much and get you so much information and assistance. Combined with a good attitude, a creative approach, and a strong reliance on hand and arm signals, interrogatives will be very helpful.

Noun—Any object, person, place, or thing (e.g., man, home, car) that can serve as the subject of a verb.

Numbers—Numbers can be very difficult, complex, and, quite honestly, boring to learn. If you simply learn the numbers, 1 through 10, then the 10s up to 100 (20, 30, etc.), and the word for 1,000, you will most likely be able to handle all you need—unless, of course, you are going to work as an accountant. You can always use a calculator or pen and paper in the office or your fingers in the market. In fact, many calculators have functions that show how to convert from one currency to another. When you're trying to get down to the nitty-gritty, this is one place to chop some time real fast and get on to more useful words that cannot be so easily substituted or signed in a pinch. A very subtle but important point to remember here is that when using your fingers to indicate numbers, be sure to study the customs of the country you are to visit. Sometimes a simple and innocent hand gesture can produce a great deal of grief in your life.

Perfective—A verb form or aspect expressing that an action was either quick and therefore momentary, or that it was or will be completed and, hence, is perfect. For example: "I read the book and then left."

Plural—More than one.

Possession—Ownership of something. This is expressed differently in various languages. For example, in English it is Joe's book. In Spanish, it would be the book of Joe. In Russian, the word *Joe* is changed to show the book belongs to him. In some languages, it might be word sequence and position or stress and intonation of the syllables that tell the status and relationship of one word to another.

Prepositions—These little words make all the difference when you begin linking nouns or pronouns (that serve as the object of the proposition) to the rest of the sentence. Examples in English are *by* and *to*. In many languages prepositions determine when you must change a word and how to do so by their rules.

Present participle (present progressive)—In English, a verb that ends in *ing* and takes a helping verb (I am running).

Pronoun—These are words that take the place of nouns and refer to nouns (e.g., I, you, he, she, it, we, they).

Singular—Just one.

Syllable—This does not mean a part of a word, as in English. In the "syllabic" languages (such as Chinese, Arabic, and Cherokee), a syllable is closer in meaning to a letter or a series of consonant-vowel groups together that make one word mean something different than another.

LEARNING TIP

Rely on synonyms to express the greatest number of ideas with the least amount of vocabulary.

Synonyms—Words that are similar (e.g., *build* and *construct*). Here is a big key: if you know the foreign word for *to construct* but want to say the word for *to build* but don't know it or can't recall it at the moment, use the word for *to construct*. It won't be perfect, but it will convey your thought and intention. Remember that the native speaker probably does not know your language and therefore will appreciate your attempt at using his. If he doesn't, he should. The point is, everyone will know that you're not a native. Perfection will come later if you care enough to work for it. Right now, just go for it and try!

Tense—The time distinctions that verbs express. In English, there are six principal tenses: present (I go), past (I went), future (I will go), present perfect (I have gone), past perfect (I had gone), and future perfect (I will have gone). Each of these has a set of progressive forms (e.g, I am going, I was going, I will be going). Various languages distinguish tenses differently.

Verb—A sentence part that indicates action (e.g., go, give, think) or links subjects with other parts of the sentence (e.g., is, was, am).

There are many more grammatical terms that you will come across, but these are most pertinent for your study. The bottom line up front (or BLUF as we call it) is this: if you use this format and fill in the blanks in the workbook pages as best you can by adapting your target language to complete the concept here, you will have what you need to function in your desired language immediately.

THE MAGIC OF TALKING BACK

A great technique for communicating is very simple: get the person to speak to you on your level. Wherever you travel, many people have probably dealt with other foreigners like yourself. Most will recognize your limitations and simplify their speech to match your ability, much as we automatically gear down to speak with a child or someone who doesn't speak English well.

However, there will always be those with whom outside contact has been minimal or who are just slow on the uptake, and they won't speak slowly or simply. There will even be some who will simply repeat the same phrase over and over, with the only change being that they say it more loudly! But, never fear, we have a method for overcoming this as well.

The most difficult part of communicating is listening/translating. So, slow the speaker down and repeat what he said in words you know to ensure that you understand what was said.

When you come across this fun and interesting dilemma, simply repeat to the person what you think he said to you, using words that you know. This puts what you are saying in the form of a simple question that requires only a yes or no answer. A nod of the head or grunt in the affirmative or negative seals the deal. For example, a man comes up to you and says some words to you and points to your car and then to an area across the street from where you are parked. You can't understand what he's saying, but your quick wit deduces that he is referring to your car and that place over there. You quickly review what he said in your mental audio recorder and recognize the words for *car, no, here,* and *there.* So, you ask him, "Car no here?" He replies, "No." You point across the street and say, "Car there, yes?" He says, "Yes." You now realize that this fellow is the local Johnny Law and you are parked in front of a hospital emergency exit. You've resolved a potentially nasty situation, as you hurry to move your car. Getting the idea? All right then, we're cooking with fire now.

PHASE 1

THE BASICS
(DAYS 1–7)

ONE DAY AT A TIME

Now that you have an idea about the terminology and tools, let's talk about how to use them and get down to the business of studying. Of course, the methodology presented here is merely my recommendation. Some students will need or want more; others, less. Adapt the methodology to meet your needs.

The objective of this book is to be generic enough to be applicable to any language. That's a tall order and, to my knowledge, has never been done. Therefore, I ask you to please understand that, as people often do, we can make generalizations (such as we all have eyes and ears and breath oxygen), but there are also exceptions—many of them. Therefore, you should look at the *concept* of what we're saying. Use your imagination in applying what you learn here. Throw out anything that doesn't work for you and modify or adopt any outside techniques that serve you well.

Now that you have an idea of how this method of study came about and your basic tools, let's talk about your study schedule. Remember that this is a general guideline here. Some of you will require a bit more time, but none should enter into this program expecting to use less. This is a commitment to yourself. *Make the time.*

I have set the goal of seven days to learn the basics and be considered functional. If you have the time and discipline to stick to the regime, you should be proficient at the end of a 30-day period using this outline.

Before we go any further, we need to clarify what we mean by the terms *functional* and *proficient*. Both are relative terms. It is *your* functionality and *your* proficiency based on what you intend to do with the language that should concern you. You must carefully define *your* needs, focus, and activities in the target language before determining functional or proficiency levels. For example, a Green Beret trainer would have different needs—and consequently a different focus—than a tourist. Identifying any special needs that you might have (e.g., knowing how to ask for directions if you are planning on driving, biking, or hiking alone) is also very important before embarking on this program.

Becoming functional depends on your individual needs, goals, and interests. The focus you choose in your study will be defined by these.

Next, you need to focus your energy on the task of learning a new language. Start every day with the language to be learned as your first thought, your priority, your mission. This focus method works for anything, so you can derive some benefit from it in other areas of your life besides language. Plus, you can study other languages after you learn the first one using this method. Think of all the benefits of being able to communicate with other people in their language and you should have ample motivation for becoming bilingual or even multilingual.

Each day use the same time quantities and sequences:

- 15 minutes reviewing everything up to that point, focusing on hard words.
- 15 minutes on five new verbs.
- 15 minutes on 15 new nouns and other supporting words.
- 10 minutes on grammar rules, with one major grammar rule per day.
- 5 minutes on five new phrases.
- 15 minutes review before you go to bed. Next to the first hour in the morning and occasional review throughout the day, this is the most important thing you can do.

When you wake up each day, try to recall as much as you can from the review the night before and then look at your work to see what you missed.

Do this every day for seven days and you'll have all you need to get started. "How is this possible?" you ask. Because I will give you the format of which words to study first. This will help tremendously and will be readily apparent once you see the list of words. You will know how they work and why it is so simple.

LEARNING LANGUAGE QUICKLY
A PRIORITIZED FLOW CHART OF ACTIVITY

- Obtain the tools for your study—notebook, pen, dictionary, and phrase book (grammar book and audio tapes/CDs are optional).

- Research your study materials and organize your study schedule.

- Write down key words and phrases.

- Prepare your flash cards.

- Label common items in the target language.

- Dedicate one solid hour of structured study per day and 15 minutes of review before going to bed.

- Study and review mentally and with the use of flash cards whenever time allows.

- Immerse yourself in the language and culture by supplementing your study with music, videos, and children's books in the native language and by eating foods from that culture.

- Methodically scan the dictionary and list words that you find useful. Focus on cognates.

- Use free association and memory tricks to help remember vocabulary.

Day 1

1. Review all your newly purchased materials for a few hours and then take a break.
2. Sit down for about half an hour and outline your book pages by category.
3. Take another couple of hours to fill in and begin each page with the appropriate headings.
4. Dig through your material to find the words and phrases you have selected and fill them in (this will require the bulk of your time in preparation).
5. Consider the basic grammar points of your language as it pertains to just the basics of sentence construction. This will make your first week of study more fruitful. Then, when you review the material thoroughly at the week's end, you'll gain even more useful insights. It will be much like a small lightning strike.
6. Use this outline to construct your book and then go by the daily schedule as your guide.

Day 2

1. Greetings, basics, and emergencies (hello, good-bye, my name is, bank, hotel, doctor, police)
2. Common expressions (How are you? How much is that?)

Day 3

1. Pronouns (I, he she; mine, your, his)
2. Key verbs (to be, to go, to eat, to buy)
3. Key nouns (house, hotel, automobile, airport)

Day 4

1. Conjunctions (and, or, but)
2. Adjectives (good, hot, rainy)
3. Adverbs (slowly, quickly, under, over)

Day 5

1. Synonyms (furious/mad; happy/glad; helpful/useful)

2. Antonyms (hot/cold; slow/fast; good/bad)
3. Numbers, time, weather (1, 2, 3; 12:00; rain, hot)
4. Commands/imperatives ("Take me to the hotel."; "Wait here for me.")

Days 6 and 7

1. Grammar—Write as much down as you can stand on day six so that you can finish the rest on day seven. Use the rest of day seven to review all your work.

   A. Past-tense rules
   B. Present-tense rules
   C. Future-tense rules
   D. Case
   E. Gender
   F. Plural and singular (number)
   G. Articles
   H. Possession

DAY 1

Day 1

I have repeated the tasks from page 27 at the beginning of each day so you won't have to flip back and forth to refresh your memory each day.

1. Review all your newly purchased materials for a few hours and then take a break.
2. Sit down for about half an hour and outline your book pages by category.
3. Take another couple of hours to fill in and begin each page with the appropriate headings.
4. Dig through your material to find the words and phrases you have selected and fill them in (this will require the bulk of your time in preparation).

5. Consider the basic grammar points of your language as it pertains to just the basics of sentence construction. This will make your first week of study more fruitful. Then, when you review the material thoroughly at the week's end, you'll gain even more useful insights.
6. Use this outline to construct your book and then go by the daily schedule as your guide. The initial day is the most difficult, both in terms of time required and the number of tasks to be accomplished.

OUTLINING YOUR NOTEBOOK

The first thing you should do is outline your notebook. (On this day you won't be filling in the phrases, just the categories in your notebook.) A good place to start is with polite words and greetings. After all, first impressions are important, and you want to be sure to know how to, at least, greet and say good-bye properly and leave people with a favorable impression. Also include basic and emergency words and phrases you might need right away. After these come common expressions, pronouns, key verbs, key nouns, conjunctions, adjectives, adverbs, synonyms, antonyms, numbers, time, weather, and commands or imperatives. Then list your rules and key grammar points.

Follow this outline and you will be off to a good start.

Common nouns are easily learned by labeling these objects around your home and office. Be sure to use easily removable stickers!

Add another hour for flash cards and one for labeling common items around the house or office. Then review the cards and labels throughout the day. Refer to your notes if you can; if not, do it in your head. Continually narrow your focus—each time you are sure you know a word, forget about it and focus on other words of the day that you are still having difficulties with.

CATEGORY

WORD/PHRASE	WORD/PHRASE IN TARGET LANGUAGE	PRONUNCIATION GUIDE

This is the basic matrix you will be using to fill in most of the words and phrases in this book. As you can see, you should fill in the category (noun, verb, greeting, emergency, etc., at the top), and then the word in English, the word in the target language, and the way you would pronounce it. You can photocopy it and use it over and over, place it in your notebook, or take it along with you as a cheat sheet. There is a blank, full-size form in the back of the book for you to make as many copies of as you like.

DAY 2

Day 2

---

1. Greetings, basics, and emergencies
2. Common expressions

You get a lot more mileage out out of the verb *to live* than the preposition *from*, which usually requires more grammar.

GREETINGS & INTRODUCTIONS

WORD/PHRASE	WORD/PHRASE IN TARGET LANGUAGE	PRONUNCIATION GUIDE
Hello		
Good-bye		
My name is		
What is your name?		
Please		
Thank you		
You're welcome		
I'm sorry		
Excuse me		
Where is (the airport, the market)?		
How do I get to (the hotel, bus station)?		
Can you show me (where, what)?		
Can you write for me (directions)?		

GREETINGS & INTRODUCTIONS

WORD/PHRASE	WORD/PHRASE IN TARGET LANGUAGE	PRONUNCIATION GUIDE
Can you draw for me (a map)?		
How do you say?		
What is (this, that)?		
Is it (near, time)?		
Are you (happy, sad, tired)?		
Do you have a car?		
I live in (the United States, England)		
My age is		
How old are you?		
Are you married?		
Where are your parents?		
When will it (happen, come)?		

GREETINGS & INTRODUCTIONS

WORD/PHRASE	WORD/PHRASE IN TARGET LANGUAGE	PRONUNCIATION GUIDE

COMMON EXPRESSIONS

This one is up to you as every country has such different colloquialisms. You should include all the ones you find interesting enough to want to either use yourself or be able to recognize. In the initial stages, try to keep them limited to useful and functional phrases. You don't need to know how to say, "Can you speak English?" If the person can, he will understand you when you ask in English!

Learn useful colloquial phrases and use them to supplement your basics to be more expressive.

Profanities

One thing I have observed is that many people will learn profanity more quickly and readily than any other aspect of a foreign language. I suggest that you skip these words altogether. The reasons are simple. First, when someone is upset with you and curses at you, you will know it by his voice and expression. You won't need (and probably don't want) to know what he's actually saying. Likewise, if the person is being sneaky and saying the words to you in jest, knowing them will only upset you. The fact is, there are very few people, despite their fluency in another language, a native speaker can't trick if that is his intention. In addition, you want to impress people with your goodness and wholesomeness.

Using obscenity does not serve you well as a foreigner, and it does not represent your homeland well. Yes, a few folks might get a kick out of it initially, but later they will view you as a bit primitive and low class. You might need these people's help later. Strange things can happen to anyone at any moment while traveling. So never be rude to anyone. You just don't know who the people might be or to whom they might be related! Instead, learn words and phrases that can serve you well. A good example is to say *what a shame* instead of *damn*. You can use this phrase anytime and never offend—and not to offend is your objective. In some countries, an offense might very well lead to imprisonment or worse. Think before you speak. This rule will help you in all things.

Jokes

Jokes can help quite a bit. If you can learn some short one-liners, these will not only help you to learn and exercise your memory, they will expand your understanding of how the foreign language works. In addition, they are a great way to make friends and cheer people up. This results in more assistance with your studies because people will want to be your friend and to help you.

Formal vs. Informal

Many languages have words that distinguish between formal and informal. That is, some verbs have a different conjugation or changing of the word to indicate if you are a friend or acquaintance with the person with whom you speak. I suggest skipping the informal altogether or at least putting it off until you are more comfortable with the language. You should be formal with everyone you first meet. Further, if you don't know the informal phrase, you won't use it, so you won't be able to offend anyone unintentionally.

Suppose in the town you are visiting the mayor befriends you to enhance his status. But if you address him informally as a peer or friend, he might suffer a great loss of face and be extremely embarrassed and upset. Remember, anyone you befriend will not be upset with you for only using formal expressions with him because he knows you are new to the language. If any person wants you to use the informal form of address, he'll let you know—and teach it to you.

COMMON EXPRESSIONS

WORD/PHRASE	WORD/PHRASE IN TARGET LANGUAGE	PRONUNCIATION GUIDE

COMMON EXPRESSIONS

WORD/PHRASE	WORD/PHRASE IN TARGET LANGUAGE	PRONUNCIATION GUIDE

DAY 3

Day 3

---

1. Pronouns
2. Key verbs
3. Key nouns

If you can learn the key nouns/pronouns and verbs for the activities you will be doing in a country, you can communicate almost anywhere.

PRONOUNS

Pronouns are handy because they make speaking easier since you don't have to keep referring to the noun and they show possession in some languages (e.g., mine, your, his).

PRONOUNS

WORD/PHRASE	WORD/PHRASE IN TARGET LANGUAGE	PRONUNCIATION GUIDE
I		
You		
She		
He		
We		
They		
Me		
Him		
Her		
Us		
Them		
My		
Your		

PRONOUNS

WORD/PHRASE	WORD/PHRASE IN TARGET LANGUAGE	PRONUNCIATION GUIDE
His		
Her		
Ours		
Their		
Mine		
Yours		
Theirs		
Myself		
Yourself		
Himself		
Herself		
Ourselves		
Themselves		

PRONOUNS

WORD/PHRASE	WORD/PHRASE IN TARGET LANGUAGE	PRONUNCIATION GUIDE
No one		
Anyone		
Someone		
Everyone		
Everything		
Anything		
Something		
Nothing		
These		
Those		
This		
That		

PRONOUNS

WORD/PHRASE	WORD/PHRASE IN TARGET LANGUAGE	PRONUNCIATION GUIDE
No one		
Anyone		

KEY VERBS

In English, the verb doesn't really change much as you change subjects: I go, you go, he goes, she goes. However, in many languages the verb changes considerably. That is why they call the verb the infinitive form, meaning before changes. For the infinitive form you add the word *to* before the verb: to go, to see. Then it is conjugated (or changed) as *he goes*. All the verbs in this section should be considered as having the word *to* in from of them.

Using this key verb short list, you should be able to communicate most of the basic actions you need. There are a few blank forms at the end of the key verb section for you to add your own verbs that do not appear on this list. Also, you can make a list of additional verbs in phase 2, "Expanding Your Vocabulary," for verbs that aren't as commonly used.

In some languages, simple commands will help (e.g., tell me, show me, take me).

There are key things that must be memorized. The trick is to know verbs and nouns; the grammar will follow. Next come adjectives and adverbs.

KEY VERBS

WORD/PHRASE	WORD/PHRASE IN TARGET LANGUAGE	PRONUNCIATION GUIDE
(To) Come		
Go		
Eat		
Drink		
Work		
Buy		
Sell		
Sleep		
Play		
Give		
Take		
Think		
Believe		

KEY VERBS

WORD/PHRASE	WORD/PHRASE IN TARGET LANGUAGE	PRONUNCIATION GUIDE
Know*		
Read		
Write		
See		
Watch		
Look		
Hear		
Listen		
Smell		
Taste		
Touch		
Make		
Do		

* Many languages have two words for this. One for people, and one for subjects.

KEY VERBS

WORD/PHRASE	WORD/PHRASE IN TARGET LANGUAGE	PRONUNCIATION GUIDE
Have		
Need		
Want		
Cost		
Break		
Learn		
Study		
Teach		
Ask		
Answer		
Repair		
Fix		
Wash		

KEY VERBS

WORD/PHRASE	WORD/PHRASE IN TARGET LANGUAGE	PRONUNCIATION GUIDE
Clean		
Put (place)		
Choose		
Happen		
Live		
Die		
Find		
Lose		
Rest		
Drive		
Fly		
Sail		
Walk		

KEY VERBS

WORD/PHRASE	WORD/PHRASE IN TARGET LANGUAGE	PRONUNCIATION GUIDE
Run		
Ride		
Stop		
Stay		
Hurry		
Understand		
Can (be able to)		
Worry		
Fear		
Fall		
Get up		
Get (obtain)		
Burn		

KEY VERBS

WORD/PHRASE	WORD/PHRASE IN TARGET LANGUAGE	PRONUNCIATION GUIDE
Hit		
Hide		
Find		
Enter		
Exit		
Send		
Receive		
Win		
Cost		
Try		
Join		
Gather		
Decide		

KEY VERBS

WORD/PHRASE	WORD/PHRASE IN TARGET LANGUAGE	PRONUNCIATION GUIDE
Desire		
Borrow		
Lend		
Owe		
Promise		
Rent		
Use		
Laugh		
Cry		
Dream		

KEY VERBS

WORD/PHRASE	WORD/PHRASE IN TARGET LANGUAGE	PRONUNCIATION GUIDE

KEY VERBS

WORD/PHRASE	WORD/PHRASE IN TARGET LANGUAGE	PRONUNCIATION GUIDE

KEY VERBS

WORD/PHRASE	WORD/PHRASE IN TARGET LANGUAGE	PRONUNCIATION GUIDE

KEY NOUNS

Learning key nouns (or the nouns that are key to your communicating) is probably the single most effective thing you can do.After all, if you can utter the word for *hotel, airport,* or *back* in the language of the country you're visiting, you have communicated what you need clearly if not grammatically.

As with the verbs, there are blank forms at the end of the key noun section for you to add your own key nouns. Also you can make a list of less common nouns in phase 2.

When you are struggling with a word, try using memory keys, such as how a word sounds or what it looks like or reminds you of. If the word for milk sounds like cat, then think: a cat drinks milk. That will cue you to the sound of the word and help you to remember it if it doesn't in fact trigger the exact word itself right away. Be creative in associating whatever the tricky word reminds you of to what that word actually means. If a word doesn't look like something to you, then listen to it . . . take a few moments, play with it. Something will click, and then you'll have it.

KEY NOUNS

WORD/PHRASE	WORD/PHRASE IN TARGET LANGUAGE	PRONUNCIATION GUIDE
Person		
Place		
Thing		
Man		
Woman		
Child		
Hotel		
House		
Restaurant		
Airport		
Bus station		
Train station		
Airplane		

KEY NOUNS

WORD/PHRASE	WORD/PHRASE IN TARGET LANGUAGE	PRONUNCIATION GUIDE
Train		
Bus		
Car		
Bicycle		
Boat		
Taxi		
Tree		
Animal		
Dog		
Cat		
Bird		
Fish		
Food		

KEY NOUNS

WORD/PHRASE	WORD/PHRASE IN TARGET LANGUAGE	PRONUNCIATION GUIDE
Water		
Meat		
Chicken		
Beef		
Pork		
Egg		
Coffee		
Milk		
Lunch		
Breakfast		
Morning		
Afternoon		
Night		

KEY NOUNS

WORD/PHRASE	WORD/PHRASE IN TARGET LANGUAGE	PRONUNCIATION GUIDE
Evening		
Day		
Week		
Month		
Year		
Telephone		
Radio		
Air Conditioner		
Bed		
Room		
Kitchen		
Bathroom/toilet		
Table		

KEY NOUNS

WORD/PHRASE	WORD/PHRASE IN TARGET LANGUAGE	PRONUNCIATION GUIDE
Chair		
Window		
Door		
Floor		
Walls		
Roof		
Ceiling		
Money		
Bank		
Market		
Garage		
Street		
Highway		

KEY NOUNS

WORD/PHRASE	WORD/PHRASE IN TARGET LANGUAGE	PRONUNCIATION GUIDE
Map		
Paper		
Pen		
Sun		
Rain		
Snow		
Clouds		
Doctor		
Medicine		
Hospital		
Dentist		
Face		
Head		

KEY NOUNS

WORD/PHRASE	WORD/PHRASE IN TARGET LANGUAGE	PRONUNCIATION GUIDE
Jaw		
Hair		
Neck		
Waist		
Stomach/abdomen		
Leg		
Foot		
Knee		
Ankle		
Thigh		
Toe		
Arm		
Hand		

KEY NOUNS

WORD/PHRASE	WORD/PHRASE IN TARGET LANGUAGE	PRONUNCIATION GUIDE
Elbow		
Finger		
Eye		
Ear		
Nose		
Mouth		
Tongue		
Tooth		
Clothing		
Shirt		
Pants		
Dress		
Underwear		

KEY NOUNS

WORD/PHRASE	WORD/PHRASE IN TARGET LANGUAGE	PRONUNCIATION GUIDE
Shoes		
Belt		
Coat		
Hat		
Laundry		
Umbrella		
Reading Glasses		
Cup		
Glass		
Plate		
Fork		
Knife		
Spoon		

KEY NOUNS

WORD/PHRASE	WORD/PHRASE IN TARGET LANGUAGE	PRONUNCIATION GUIDE
Napkin		
Bath		
Sink/faucet		
Blanket		
Pillow		
Book		
Office		
Building		
Color		
White		
Black		
Gray		
Yellow		

KEY NOUNS

WORD/PHRASE	WORD/PHRASE IN TARGET LANGUAGE	PRONUNCIATION GUIDE
Orange		
Red		
Blue		
Green		
Gold		
Silver		
Shape		
Circle		
Square		
Box		
Rectangle		
Triangle		
Height		

KEY NOUNS

WORD/PHRASE	WORD/PHRASE IN TARGET LANGUAGE	PRONUNCIATION GUIDE
Weight		
Texture		

KEY NOUNS

WORD/PHRASE	WORD/PHRASE IN TARGET LANGUAGE	PRONUNCIATION GUIDE

KEY NOUNS

WORD/PHRASE	WORD/PHRASE IN TARGET LANGUAGE	PRONUNCIATION GUIDE

KEY NOUNS

WORD/PHRASE	WORD/PHRASE IN TARGET LANGUAGE	PRONUNCIATION GUIDE

DAY 4

Day 4

---

1. Conjunctions
2. Adjectives
3. Adverbs

As you recall, conjunctions are the joining words. In English, there are basically two types of conjunctions. Coordinating conjunctions (and, or, if, but) connect sentences, clauses, phrases or words. Subordinating conjunctions (although, because, after) introduce dependent (or subordinate) clauses.

CONJUNCTIONS

WORD/PHRASE	WORD/PHRASE IN TARGET LANGUAGE	PRONUNCIATION GUIDE
And		
Or		
If		
But		
Nor		
With		
Unless		
Before		
Although		
However		
As		
Since		
Therefore		

CONJUNCTIONS

WORD/PHRASE	WORD/PHRASE IN TARGET LANGUAGE	PRONUNCIATION GUIDE
Because		
Whether		
Until		
In order that		
As soon as		
As long as		
Now that		

CONJUNCTIONS

WORD/PHRASE	WORD/PHRASE IN TARGET LANGUAGE	PRONUNCIATION GUIDE

ADJECTIVES

Adjectives turn plain nouns into descriptive ones, adding color and detail to speech. In English, adjectives can come before the noun or after the linking verb (the *beautiful* sunset; the sunset was *beautiful*), but both still modify the noun, *sunset*. Their placement varies with other languages.

There are three things that you can do to make learning adjectives easier:

1. Learn the suffixes that turn words into adjectives in the target language. These suffixes are usually listed in the appropriate section in a grammar book. The make building words from root stems very easy.
2. Learn the comparative and superlative forms of adjectives (good, better, best).
3. Learn adjectives in opposites for easier retention (hot, cold). (More on this in the section on antonyms.)

ADJECTIVES

WORD/PHRASE	WORD/PHRASE IN TARGET LANGUAGE	PRONUNCIATION GUIDE
Good/bad		
High/low		
Large/small		
Thick/thin		
Same/different		
Light/dark		
Light/heavy		
Full/empty		
Hot/cold		
Pretty/ugly		
Warm/cool		
Many/few		
Short/long		

ADJECTIVES

WORD/PHRASE	WORD/PHRASE IN TARGET LANGUAGE	PRONUNCIATION GUIDE
First/last		
Above/below		
Ahead/behind		
In/out		
Happy/sad		
Fast/slow		
Easy/difficult		
Hard/soft		
Wet/dry		
Smooth/rough		
Tight/loose		
Far/near		
Young/old		

ADJECTIVES

WORD/PHRASE	WORD/PHRASE IN TARGET LANGUAGE	PRONUNCIATION GUIDE
Weak/strong		
Left/right		
Up/down		
Under/over		
Rich/poor		

ADJECTIVES

WORD/PHRASE	WORD/PHRASE IN TARGET LANGUAGE	PRONUNCIATION GUIDE

ADJECTIVES

WORD/PHRASE	WORD/PHRASE IN TARGET LANGUAGE	PRONUNCIATION GUIDE

ADJECTIVES

WORD/PHRASE	WORD/PHRASE IN TARGET LANGUAGE	PRONUNCIATION GUIDE

ADJECTIVES

WORD/PHRASE	WORD/PHRASE IN TARGET LANGUAGE	PRONUNCIATION GUIDE

ADVERBS

An adverb typically modifies a verb, an adjective, another adverb, a preposition, a phrase, a clause, or a sentence. Adverbs typically express quality, place, time, degree, number, cause, opposition, affirmation, or denial. In English, the same word can often function as an adverb or adjective, such as high (the plane is high; the plane flew high). Adverbs can also serve to connect, and their function is sometimes confused with that of a preposition.

As with adjectives, the learning of adverbs can be furthered in three ways:

1. Learn the suffixes that turn words into adverbs. In English, adverbs are often formed by adding *ly* to an adjective (slow + ly = slowly).
2. Learn the comparative and superlative forms of adverbs (quickly, more quickly, most quickly).
3. Learn adverbs in opposite pairs when applicable for greater efficiency (quickly / slowly).

ADVERBS

WORD/PHRASE	WORD/PHRASE IN TARGET LANGUAGE	PRONUNCIATION GUIDE
Inside/Outside		
Opposite/beside		
Through		
Away		
Now/later		
Probably		
Possibly		
Rather		
Instead		
Between		
About		
Only		
Again		

ADVERBS

WORD/PHRASE	WORD/PHRASE IN TARGET LANGUAGE	PRONUNCIATION GUIDE
Very		
Never/Always		
Together		
Above all		
At last		
Little		
Perhaps		
Each		
Some		
Slowly/quickly		
Fairly/unfairly (or fair/unfair)		
Cheaply/costly		
Rarely/often		

ADVERBS

WORD/PHRASE	WORD/PHRASE IN TARGET LANGUAGE	PRONUNCIATION GUIDE
Early/late		
Straight		
Fast/slow		
Bright		
Close		
Deep		
Direct		
Even		
First/last		
Hard/soft		
High/low		
Loud		
Quick		

ADVERBS

WORD/PHRASE	WORD/PHRASE IN TARGET LANGUAGE	PRONUNCIATION GUIDE
Right/left Right/wrong		
Rough/smooth		
Sharp		
Tight/loose		
Here/there		
Everywhere/nowhere		
Anywhere		
Somewhere		
Never/always		
Today/tomorrow/ yesterday		
More/less		

ADVERBS

WORD/PHRASE	WORD/PHRASE IN TARGET LANGUAGE	PRONUNCIATION GUIDE

ADVERBS

WORD/PHRASE	WORD/PHRASE IN TARGET LANGUAGE	PRONUNCIATION GUIDE

ADVERBS

WORD/PHRASE	WORD/PHRASE IN TARGET LANGUAGE	PRONUNCIATION GUIDE

PREPOSITIONS

In some languages, including English, prepositions connect a noun, a pronoun, or a noun phrase to a verb (she drove *by* me), to a noun (the smell *of* fresh bread), or to an adjective (old *in* age). As you can see, many of the prepositions listed here can also function as adverbs in English, and that is true in other languages as well. So you have to note the word's use in a sentence to know whether it is functioning as an adverb or preposition.

PREPOSITIONS

WORD/PHRASE	WORD/PHRASE IN TARGET LANGUAGE	PRONUNCIATION GUIDE
For		
In		
At		
By		
To		
On		
From		
With		
Within		
Among		
Around		
During		
Except for		

PREPOSITIONS

WORD/PHRASE	WORD/PHRASE IN TARGET LANGUAGE	PRONUNCIATION GUIDE
Inside		
Opposite		
Beside		
Through		
Toward		
Unless		
While		
Instead of		
According to		
Between		
Against		
About		

PREPOSITIONS

WORD/PHRASE	WORD/PHRASE IN TARGET LANGUAGE	PRONUNCIATION GUIDE

DAY 5

Day 5

---

1. Synonyms
2. Antonyms
3. Numbers, time, weather
4. Commands/imperatives

Beginning with day five we leave the primary parts of a sentence and go on to other nuances of language that can make learning a language either easier or harder for you, depending on the language itself and the way you approach it. My approach stresses learning only what you really need to know, based on your individual needs, and the simple rules that apply most of the time.

SYNONYMS

As stated in the "Key Words for Words" section, synonyms are words that are similar in meaning. Though differences may exist, they are so subtle as to be imperceptible to most people. We talked about synonyms when we were listing adjectives and adverbs, but synonyms can be nouns, pronouns, and verbs as well as adjectives or adverbs.

Anytime you find a synonym that is easier for you to remember than the real word you are searching for, substitute it. You'll probably be close enough in meaning to get your point across. If your grammar book has a section for synonyms, use them to add to the your collection for memorization on the following pages or in your notebook.

SYNONYMS

WORD/PHRASE	WORD/PHRASE IN TARGET LANGUAGE	PRONUNCIATION GUIDE
Road/route		
Country/nation		
City/town		
Work/labor		
Market/store		
Automobile/car		
Medium/average		
Large/big		
Happy/glad		
Angry/mad		
Restaurant/cafe		

SYNONYMS

WORD/PHRASE	WORD/PHRASE IN TARGET LANGUAGE	PRONUNCIATION GUIDE

SYNONYMS

WORD/PHRASE	WORD/PHRASE IN TARGET LANGUAGE	PRONUNCIATION GUIDE

SYNONYMS

WORD/PHRASE	WORD/PHRASE IN TARGET LANGUAGE	PRONUNCIATION GUIDE

ANTONYMS

Antonyms are the opposite of synonyms—they are words with opposite meanings (hot/cold). As with synonyms, antonyms can be nouns, pronouns, and verbs, as well as adjectives and adverbs.

Always try to learn your words in pairs and you double your retention. For example, if you need to know the word for *to draw*, you should also look up the word for *to erase*.

We have already listed may antonyms in the adjective and adverb section, but use the following pages to record other pairs that you may need in your travels. Or you can list them in your notebook.

ANTONYMS

WORD/PHRASE	WORD/PHRASE IN TARGET LANGUAGE	PRONUNCIATION GUIDE
Friend/enemy		
Late/early		
Hot/cold		
Good/bad		
Peace/war		
Friendly/mean		
Clean/dirty		
Agree/disagree		
Pleased/displeased		
Tired/rested		

ANTONYMS

WORD/PHRASE	WORD/PHRASE IN TARGET LANGUAGE	PRONUNCIATION GUIDE

ANTONYMS

WORD/PHRASE	WORD/PHRASE IN TARGET LANGUAGE	PRONUNCIATION GUIDE

NUMBERS, TIME, WEATHER

These are standard categories that every one focuses on. I put them here as a matter of protocol for those who want to learn them. However, I encourage you to ask yourself, "When was the last time I asked anyone for the time, what date it is, or how the weather is?" The weather words alone can kill ya. I say skip 'em, but if you don't want to, look up the ones you think are *essential* to your travels and include just those.

NUMBERS

WORD/PHRASE	WORD/PHRASE IN TARGET LANGUAGE	PRONUNCIATION GUIDE
1 (one)		
2 (two)		
3 (three)		
4 (four)		
5 (five)		
6 (six)		
7 (seven)		
8 (eight)		
9 (nine)		
10 (ten)		

TIME

WORD/PHRASE	WORD/PHRASE IN TARGET LANGUAGE	PRONUNCIATION GUIDE

WEATHER

WORD/PHRASE	WORD/PHRASE IN TARGET LANGUAGE	PRONUNCIATION GUIDE

COMMANDS/IMPERATIVES

You might need these for emphasis, especially with taxi drivers or other insistent vendors or service providers. Look up the rules for the language you wish to learn. If they are too complex, skip 'em. Just write down the key ones such as Stop!

COMMANDS/IMPERATIVES

WORD/PHRASE	WORD/PHRASE IN TARGET LANGUAGE	PRONUNCIATION GUIDE
Stop!		
Go!		
Take me to the hotel.		
Bring me the check.		
Wait here.		
Don't do that.		
Shut up.		
Answer me.		

COMMANDS/IMPERATIVES

WORD/PHRASE	WORD/PHRASE IN TARGET LANGUAGE	PRONUNCIATION GUIDE

COMMANDS/IMPERATIVES

WORD/PHRASE	WORD/PHRASE IN TARGET LANGUAGE	PRONUNCIATION GUIDE

DAYS 6 AND 7

Days 6 and 7

1. Grammar—Write as much down as you can stand on day six so that you can finish the rest on day seven. Use the rest of day seven to review all your work.

    A. Past-tense rules
    B. Present-tense rules
    C. Future-tense rules
    D. Case
    E. Gender
    F. Plural and singular (number)
    G. Articles
    H   Possession

GRAMMAR

Learn to conjugate helping verbs (to be, to do, to have, to want) and use them with infinitives and gerunds to avoid having to conjugate every verb.

This is where it starts getting tougher, where you stop memorizing words and start learning something about the mechanics of the target language and why you make certain changes to indicate tense, case, gender, plurals, and possession Again, remember that how much grammar you should learn depends on the level of functionality or proficiency in the language you need to accomplish your mission.

PAST-TENSE RULES

After present tense, probably the one you will use most often is past tense. Most of the time in English this is simple: *work, worked*. However, there are exceptions; these are called irregular verbs. *See* becomes *saw* in past tense. For these verbs (which it seems are always the most commonly used ones in any language), you have to list them and learn the various tenses. Learn as many as you can right away. The rest will come to you as you refer to your easy-reference chart.

If you don't want to learn the various forms of irregular verbs, you have a couple of options.

1. You can learn the rule for using helping or auxiliary verbs with the infinitive form of the verb (especially of to do) and use it whenever possible. For instance, *I saw* can be said with almost identical meaning as *I did see*.
2. You can try the little trick of using past participle with the helping verb *have* or *be* or both (she has looked or she has been looking). In most languages, participles are easily created for regular verbs. In English you usually add *ed* to the

end of the word to form the past participle (work/worked). Other languages have different rules, but once you learn them, it's much easier than learning how to conjugate every verb.

3. Even if it leaves a little to be desired in terms of grammar, you can always add an adverb to a sentence to indicate tense (e.g., "I buy yesterday" or "I pay next week" isn't correct, but it gets the point across).

Of course, not all languages will have all three options, but almost all will have at least one. If you learn to just one of these tricks, you'll master past tense in little time. Choose whichever option is easiest for you. As I noted earlier, the key to mastering a language (or any task, for that matter) is to use tried-and-true principles, and these are.

If you learn to conjugate only three verbs (to be, to do, to go) properly, in past, present, and future tense for all your pronouns, you will be able to say almost anything you will ever need—if not perfectly, then at least clearly. The reason this works is that because in almost every single language, when two verbs are used together, you don't conjugate the second verb. If you can only learn to conjugate one verb correctly, choose "I did."

PAST TENSE TO BE

PRONOUN	WORD/ PHRASE	WORD/PHRASE IN TARGET LANGUAGE	PRONUNCIATION GUIDE
I	was		
You	were		
You (f, formal)	were		
He	was		
She	was		
It	was		
We	were		
You (p, plural)	were		
They	were		

PAST TENSE TO DO

PRONOUN	WORD/PHRASE	WORD/PHRASE IN TARGET LANGUAGE	PRONUNCIATION GUIDE
I	did		
You	did		
You (f)	did		
He	did		
She	did		
It	did		
We	did		
You (p)	did		
They	did		

PAST TENSE TO GO

PRONOUN	WORD/ PHRASE	WORD/PHRASE IN TARGET LANGUAGE	PRONUNCIATION GUIDE
I	went		
You	went		
You (f)	went		
He	went		
She	went		
It	went		
We	went		
You (p)	went		
They	went		

PAST TENSE TO HAVE

PRONOUN	WORD/ PHRASE	WORD/PHRASE IN TARGET LANGUAGE	PRONUNCIATION GUIDE
I	had		
You	had		
You (f)	had		
He	had		
She	had		
It	had		
We	had		
You (p)	had		
They	had		

PAST TENSE TO WANT

PRONOUN	WORD/ PHRASE	WORD/PHRASE IN TARGET LANGUAGE	PRONUNCIATION GUIDE
I	wanted		
You	wanted		
You (f)	wanted		
He	wanted		
She	wanted		
It	wanted		
We	wanted		
You (p)	wanted		
They	wanted		

PAST TENSE TO SEE

PRONOUN	WORD/ PHRASE	WORD/PHRASE IN TARGET LANGUAGE	PRONUNCIATION GUIDE
I	saw		
You	saw		
You (f)	saw		
He	saw		
She	saw		
It	saw		
We	saw		
You (p)	saw		
They	saw		

PAST TENSE TO BE ABLE

PRONOUN	WORD/ PHRASE	WORD/PHRASE IN TARGET LANGUAGE	PRONUNCIATION GUIDE
I	can		
You	can		
You (f)	can		
He	can		
She	can		
It	can		
We	can		
You (p)	can		
They	can		

PAST TENSE TO MAKE

PRONOUN	WORD/ PHRASE	WORD/PHRASE IN TARGET LANGUAGE	PRONUNCIATION GUIDE
I	made		
You	made		
You (f)	made		
He	made		
She	made		
It	made		
We	made		
You (p)	made		
They	made		

PAST TENSE TO NEED

PRONOUN	WORD/ PHRASE	WORD/PHRASE IN TARGET LANGUAGE	PRONUNCIATION GUIDE
I	needed		
You	needed		
You (f)	needed		
He	needed		
She	needed		
It	needed		
We	needed		
You (p)	needed		
They	needed		

PRESENT-TENSE RULES

Much of the same applies to present tense. If you know how to conjugate the magic three verbs (to be, to do, to go) properly in present tense, then you can say most anything you need: I am happy, I do work, I go to work.

There is also a nice trick you can do with present tense: use the present participle and you won't have to conjugate different verbs. In English, the present participle is formed by using a helping verb and adding *ing* to the main verb (I am reading). Other languages may form the present participle in different ways or call it something else.

PRESENT TENSE TO BE

PRONOUN	WORD/ PHRASE	WORD/PHRASE IN TARGET LANGUAGE	PRONUNCIATION GUIDE
I	am		
You	are		
You (f)	are		
He	is		
She	is		
It	is		
We	are		
You (p)	are		
They	are		

PRESENT PARTICIPLE TO BE

PRONOUN	WORD/ PHRASE	WORD/PHRASE IN TARGET LANGUAGE	PRONUNCIATION GUIDE
I	am being		
You	are being		
You (f)	are being		
He	is being		
She	is being		
It	is being		
We	are being		
You (p)	are being		
They	are being		

PRESENT TENSE TO GO

PRONOUN	WORD/ PHRASE	WORD/PHRASE IN TARGET LANGUAGE	PRONUNCIATION GUIDE
I	go		
You	go		
You (f)	go		
He	goes		
She	goes		
It	goes		
We	go		
You (p)	go		
They	go		

PRESENT PARTICIPLE TO GO

PRONOUN	WORD/ PHRASE	WORD/PHRASE IN TARGET LANGUAGE	PRONUNCIATION GUIDE
I	am going		
You	are going		
You (f)	are going		
He	is going		
She	is going		
It	is going		
We	are going		
You (p)	are going		
They	are going		

PRESENT TENSE TO HAVE

PRONOUN	WORD/PHRASE	WORD/PHRASE IN TARGET LANGUAGE	PRONUNCIATION GUIDE
I	have		
You	have		
You (f)	have		
He	has		
She	has		
It	has		
We	have		
You (p)	have		
They	have		

PRESENT TENSE TO WANT

PRONOUN	WORD/ PHRASE	WORD/PHRASE IN TARGET LANGUAGE	PRONUNCIATION GUIDE
I	want		
You	want		
You (f)	want		
He	wants		
She	wants		
It	wants		
We	want		
You (p)	want		
They	want		

PRESENT TENSE TO SEE

PRONOUN	WORD/ PHRASE	WORD/PHRASE IN TARGET LANGUAGE	PRONUNCIATION GUIDE
I	see		
You	see		
You (f)	see		
He	sees		
She	sees		
It	sees		
We	see		
You (p)	see		
They	see		

PRESENT TENSE TO BE ABLE

PRONOUN	WORD/ PHRASE	WORD/PHRASE IN TARGET LANGUAGE	PRONUNCIATION GUIDE
I	can		
You	can		
You (f)	can		
He	can		
She	can		
It	can		
We	can		
You (p)	can		
They	can		

PRESENT TENSE TO MAKE

PRONOUN	WORD/ PHRASE	WORD/PHRASE IN TARGET LANGUAGE	PRONUNCIATION GUIDE
I	make		
You	make		
You (f)	make		
He	makes		
She	makes		
It	makes		
We	make		
You (p)	make		
They	make		

PRESENT TENSE NEED

PRONOUN	WORD/ PHRASE	WORD/PHRASE IN TARGET LANGUAGE	PRONUNCIATION GUIDE
I	need		
You	need		
You (f)	need		
He	needs		
She	needs		
It	needs		
We	need		
You (p)	need		
They	need		

FUTURE-TENSE RULES

As with the two primary tenses, you must ascertain which form of the future tense is the easiest for you to use. For example, in Spanish there are actually 17 cases. Many natives don't even know them all or how to use them properly. It's sad to say, but much the same is true in English. Most of us do not use correct English. The point is to find the form of future case verb rules that are easiest for you and write them down here. Do not worry if it is not perfectly correct.

The fact that you saying the verb in a future form will convey your intention and serve your purposes. In English, using the future tense makes conjugation very easy: I will go, he will go, she will go, they will go—everyone will go! But not all languages are quite this easy. After you learn how to form the future tense you can add a time frame to make your intentions more specific and clarify any misconceptions your sentence structure might have created (e.g., I will work tomorrow).

Learn I will and put this with the infinitive to solve most of your your problems.

FUTURE TENSE TO BE

PRONOUN	WORD/ PHRASE	WORD/PHRASE IN TARGET LANGUAGE	PRONUNCIATION GUIDE
I	will be		
You	will be		
You (f)	will be		
He	will be		
She	will be		
It	will be		
We	will be		
You (p)	will be		
They	will be		

FUTURE TENSE TO DO

PRONOUN	WORD/PHRASE	WORD/PHRASE IN TARGET LANGUAGE	PRONUNCIATION GUIDE
I	will do		
You	will do		
You (f)	will do		
He	will do		
She	will do		
It	will do		
We	will do		
You (p)	will do		
They	will do		

PRESENT TENSE TO MAKE

PRONOUN	WORD/ PHRASE	WORD/PHRASE IN TARGET LANGUAGE	PRONUNCIATION GUIDE
I	will make		
You	will make		
You (f)	will make		
He	will make		
She	will make		
It	will make		
We	will make		
You (p)	will make		
They	will make		

FUTURE TENSE TO WANT

PRONOUN	WORD/ PHRASE	WORD/PHRASE IN TARGET LANGUAGE	PRONUNCIATION GUIDE
I	will want		
You	will want		
You (f)	will want		
He	will want		
She	will want		
It	will want		
We	will want		
You (p)	will want		
They	will want		

FUTURE TENSE TO BE ABLE

PRONOUN	WORD/ PHRASE	WORD/PHRASE IN TARGET LANGUAGE	PRONUNCIATION GUIDE
I	will be able to		
You	will be able to		
You (f)	will be able to		
He	will be able to		
She	will be able to		
It	will be able to		
We	will be able to		
You (p)	will be able to		
They	will be able to		

FUTURE TENSE TO NEED

PRONOUN	WORD/ PHRASE	WORD/PHRASE IN TARGET LANGUAGE	PRONUNCIATION GUIDE
I	will need		
You	will need		
You (f)	will need		
He	will need		
She	will need		
It	will need		
We	will need		
You (p)	will need		
They	will need		

FUTURE TENSE (FILL IN VERB)

PRONOUN	WORD/PHRASE	WORD/PHRASE IN TARGET LANGUAGE	PRONUNCIATION GUIDE
I	will		
You	will		
You (f)	will		
He	will		
She	will		
It	will		
We	will		
You (p)	will		
They	will		

FUTURE TENSE (FILL IN VERB)

PRONOUN	WORD/ PHRASE	WORD/PHRASE IN TARGET LANGUAGE	PRONUNCIATION GUIDE
I	will		
You	will		
You (f)	will		
He	will		
She	will		
It	will		
We	will		
You (p)	will		
They	will		

A FINAL NOTE ON VERBS

You might want to consider making your verb lists so that all that is important is together on one page if possible so that it is easier for you to carry, reference, and study. Consolidating alone often tends to help you put things in relational perspective, which contributes to ease in memorization.

CASE

There are just no two ways about it. Case is probably the toughest aspect of learning another language because case really doesn't play that much of a role in English.

Case is the aspect of grammar that involves the inflection of nouns, pronouns, and adjectives that denotes the syntactic relation of these words to others in the sentence. In English, we normally use a word (such as a preposition) to indicate the relationship between words. For example, we would say, "I give that *to* you." In another language, such as Spanish, there is a rule that changes the verb to imply both the preposition and the noun or pronoun receiving the action. For example, in the phrase *I give to you*, the word that changes is *you*. The way the word changes is called the case. The rules might change depending on whether the word is singular or plural, whether the word is used as a direct object or an indirect object, or some other factor. Therefore, in a foreign language there could be many variations of one simple noun, instead of using one preposition or conjunction and one verb conjugation and tense.

Foreign languages often change all the adjectives to match the gender and number according to the rules of that case. This makes learning some languages challenging. If your target language has these complex rules for case, just accept the parameters and do the best you can. Fortunately, only a few of the most difficult languages for English speakers have these case rules. Just do your best to learn the case as you learn your key verbs and use them the best you can.

Don't be intimidated. Remember that many natives don't speak perfectly, and they don't expect you to. As we keep emphasizing, the important thing is to learn your key nouns and verbs and you will do fine.

GENDER

This is an obvious and important element of any language, but it is not critical to master. Most of the time, you'll know when you make a gender mistake by the shy or embarrassed chuckles you elicit. Try to learn the gender of the important nouns when you learn the noun itself. Many times this will be in the form of an article, pronoun, or adjective.

NUMBER

Number refers to whether a word is singular or plural. These are generally very easy to learn in most languages.

ARTICLES

In English, the articles are *a, an*, and *the*. Some languages use articles and some don't. If the language you are studying does, write them down and memorize them. Be sure to learn the rules for when the word is plural, feminine, or masculine. Some articles have feminine and masculine derivatives.

POSSESSION

Simple rules usually apply here. As we discussed in the section on pronouns, possession is sometimes shown by the use of a possessive pronoun (*his* book). It might also be indicated by the use of an apostrophe and an *s* added to a word (John's book), or a prepositional phrase (the book of John). In some languages it might involve the case rule of changing the noun to indicate its possession of an item.

Write down all the rules of possession in your target language. Review and select the easiest for you to learn. Summarize and make this part of your daily grammar review.

* * *

That's the end of phase one. Be sure to review all your basics for 15 minutes everyday before you begin phase two. The words and phrases from the first week are the most important tools you'll need, and you must have them as your active vocabulary. That means you must know them inside out because they are what you will pull from every time you need to communicate, whether you're ini-tiating or responding to communication.

PHASE 2

EXPANDING YOUR VOCABULARY (DAYS 8–30)

ADDING NEW WORDS AND PHRASES

Now that you have finished the basics, you should be functional in your target language. Or at least as functional as you need to be as determined by your specific needs and focus. Now is the time to move on to expanding your vocab-ulary by learning new words and phrases, as well as to tackle some of the complexities and nuances of the language that you didn't bother with in phase one.

This phase is less structured than phase one. About the only specific daily tasks I suggest here are continuing your daily cumulative reviews and tackling the letters of the alpha-bet to incorporate new words into your vocabulary, as we have already discussed. You have approximately

22 days (days 8 through 30). (Hopefully, you didn't start your study in February—in which case you have only 20 days to cram!) In the Romanized alphabet (A through Z), you have 26 letters, so you'll have to double up on a few days.

As we have already discussed, if your target language does not use the Romanized alphabet, you can divide your study into areas of activity, such as accommodations, transportation, dining out, socializing, shopping, sight-seeing, etc. Try to come up with one heading for each day remaining in the month.

Learn the words and phrases you think you will need in addition to the key ones you learned in phase one. Also learn any rules (e.g., for gender or case or conjugation) that apply as you learn the the the new words or phrases.

CREATING YOUR OWN CHEAT SHEET

One last thing before you head out into the world to try your new language skills: a cheat sheet. Create an easy-reference sheet on one page (or back and front) of all the key words and phrases you think you will need most. The order that you list the key items is also up to you. Just make sure that you can glance at it and find what you need quickly.

Cheat sheets are very personal. What works for a tourist interested in sight-seeing and recreation won't be that useful for a businessman. And a bicyclist or backpacker would have comletely different needs from someone who's staying in a hotel in the middle of a city.

Because you will use this a lot, at least at first, you might want to have it laminated so it will last.

Another idea is to have a series of small cheat sheets for different occasions. For example, you might have a laminated card for dining out, another for getting around, and another for business customs. That way you could take just the ones you needed for your various excursions.

You might also take a tip from smart travelers who don't speak the language of the country they're visiting. They often have a native speaker write out a card or sheet of paper for them saying something like, "Take me to the Shangri-La Hotel," or "Take me to the Golden Lotus restaurant," with them before they venture out. That way they can just show the card to a taxi driver and get to their destination easily. You could prepare a series of emergency cards like this to meet your needs, whatever they might be. In any language, it's best to be prepared.

* * *

That's it. It sounds like a lot, and it is. Learning a language involves a lot of work. Many of us spend our entire lives learning even our native tongue.

Don't be frustrated or intimidated. Just follow the steps outlined in this book. Take it bit-by-bit, day-by-day, step-by-step. Each part will make sense alone and will contribute to the whole. Always refer to the down-and-dirty parts to get the real gist real fast, and your growing confidence will encourage you to fill in between as you go.

Good luck and write to me in care of the publisher and let me know what you think of this method as well as any suggestions you have.

RECOMMENDED RESOURCES

To help make your study more effective, I will recommend some books and other items of help.

1. Barrons books seem to me to be the best because they are the closest to my system. However, even these guides still spend a lot of time on unimportant phrases and nonessential methods that make you learn things that are readily apparent to you or that you'll never need. It is their nicely simplistic breakdown of grammar rules, the categorization of subjects, and the commonly used words minidictionaries that make them worthy of your attention—and your funds.

2. Berlitz books are generally pretty good as well. However, for some reason, Berlitz doesn't apply the same formula to all of its books. So, do some comparative analysis of its books for your specific language before you buy. After reading this guide, you'll know what you're looking for and how to choose the best book for you.

3. Both Barron and Berlitz use similar methods, so the key here is the language itself. As you browse through the Barron and Berlitz books, select the one that offers the simplest phrases for you to use as replies. Also look for the best breakdowns of synonyms and antonyms because these will get you further faster.

4. The other guides are all right in general, but they often leave you with more questions than answers. With some of the more exotic, non-Latin-based languages, you're going to have to go with whatever you can get your hands on. If your local bookstores don't offer much, and their clerks can't get you anything promising . . . then try accessing the Internet before settling for whatever they have to offer. In some cases, there might very well be only one book in some rare language.

   If you run across this, try to get some tapes, CDs, movies, music of the language, whatever you can and use them as described earlier. Those tapes that ask you to memorize long phrases or learn phrases with little changes in them (e.g., he said, she said, I said) aren't as good. Remember, you're paying for the tape and its time is limited—you need those things in the first-person singular. If it's all you can get, take it. Also, those that repeat the same sentence more than once are wasting your money because they are cutting in half what they could put on the tape for you. That's why they make a stop and rewind button. You'll need them. Use them.

5. Another method for getting a study guide or tape is to get someone you know who can write and speak the language to make one for you. For an audiotape, provide your vol-

unteer speaker with a recorder and tape, pay him whatever you two agree on (maybe dinner or such), and have him read English words followed by the corresponding word in the foreign language into the tape recorder. This way you are creating your own tailor-made tape with exactly what you need.

Likewise, you can make a written guide by having the person write the foreign words (better to print) beside the list of words you have copied from this guide. Then, after he has gone through the list and written the foreign words beside your English ones, you can read it to him. Have the person correct you and then write down how the correct pronunciation of that word sounds to your ears. This will give you a great guide to study and will have you speaking more correctly and quickly. You can also use your tailor-made guide as a point-and-show reference chart when you are traveling in that country. When your pronunciation is not close enough for someone to understand what you're saying, just point to the word you're trying to convey. Your partner can read it, and soon you'll be all sorted out.

LEARNING TIPS

1. Watch movies, read children's books, listen to music, and go to restaurants to get an insight into the culture and nuances of your target language.

2. A really neat trick for learning the grammar of another language is to do just like children do—get a kids' grammar book for that language. Grammar will tell you how to put the sentences together the way they do, as well as those little things you need to know for each group of words such as tense, case, and conjugation.

3. Learning adjectives and adverbs is greatly enhanced by studying them in antonym pairs.

4. Learn to use cognates to maximize your usable vocabulary.

5. Rely on synonyms to express the greatest number of ideas with the least amount of vocabulary.

6. The most difficult part of communicating is listening/translating. So, slow the speaker down and repeat what he said in words you know to ensure that you understand what was said.

7. Becoming functional depends on your individual needs, goals, and interests. The focus you choose in your study will be defined by these.

8. Common nouns are easily learned by labeling these objects around your home and office.

9. You get a lot more mileage out of the verb *to live* than the preposition *from*, which usually requires more grammar.

10. Learn useful colloquial phrases and use them to supplement your basics to be more expressive.

11. In some languages, simple commands will help (e.g., tell me, show me, take me).

12. When you are struggling with a word, try using memory keys, such as how a word sounds or what it looks like or reminds you of.

13. Learn to conjugate helping verbs (to be, to do, to have, to want) and use them with infinitives and gerunds to avoid conjugating every verb.

14. If you learn to conjugate only three verbs (to be, to do, to go) properly, in past, present, and future tense for all your pronouns, you will be able to say almost anything you will ever need—if not perfectly, then at least clearly. The reason this works is because in almost every single language, when two verbs are used together, you don't conjugate the second verb. If you can only learn to conjugate one verb correctly, choose "I did."

15. A nice trick to do with present tense: use the present participle and you won't have to conjugate different verbs. In English, the present participle is formed by using a helping verb and adding *ing* to the main verb (I *am* read-*ing*). Other languages may form the present participle in different ways or call it something else, but they all have a similar shortcut you can use.

16. Learn *I will* and put this with the infinitive (to + a verb, as explained in the section on verbs) to solve most of your problems (I will meet).

APPENDIX: REPRODUCIBLE FORMS

On the following two pages are the workbook forms that were used throughout this book. The first form is useful for words and phrases the second is intended to help with conjugation of verbs. You can photocopy these forms, and then fill in the category at the top—e.g., key nouns, verb to be conjugated, or letter of the alphabet (or situation for non-Latin based languages) for that day's vocabulary expansion. If you wish, you can place the forms in your notebook and fill them out on the days indicated in the book.

CATEGORY:

WORD/PHRASE	WORD/PHRASE IN TARGET LANGUAGE	PRONUCIATION GUIDE

VERB TO BE CONJUGATED:

PRONOUN	VERB OR VERB PHRASE	VERB/PHRASE IN TARGET LANGUAGE	PRONUCIATION GUIDE
I			
You			
You (f)			
He			
She			
It			
We			
You (p)			
They			

PRONOUN	VERB OR VERB PHRASE	VERB/PHRASE IN TARGET LANGUAGE	PRONUNCIATION GUIDE
You			
You (pl)			
He			
She			
It			
We			
You (pl)			
They			

ABOUT THE AUTHOR

Mykel Hawke is a retired Special Forces Combat Commander, formerly a Green Beret Senior Sergeant in Medicine, Communications, and Intelligence with a bachelor's degree in Biology & a master's degree in Psychology. He also obtained black belts in Aikido and Judo.

Myke's lived & taught survival for two decades and been in nine conflicts, but Hawke's better known for TV shows about survival and special ops, books on Survival, language and other subjects, as well as designing Hawke Brand Survival & SOF products.